wonder.land

Moira Buffini's plays include *Blavatsky's Tower* (Machine Room), *Gabriel* (Soho Theatre), *Silence* (Birmingham Rep), *Loveplay* (Royal Shakespeare Company), *Dinner* (National Theatre and West End), *Dying for It*, adapted from *The Suicide* by Nikolai Erdman (Almeida), *A Vampire Story* (NT Connections), *Marianne Dreams* (Almeida), *Welcome to Thebes* (National Theatre) and *Handbagged* (Tricycle Theatre).

MOIRA BUFFINI

wonder.land

Created by
DAMON ALBARN
MOIRA BUFFINI
RUFUS NORRIS

Music by
DAMON ALBARN

Book and lyrics by
MOIRA BUFFINI

Inspired by
Alice's Adventures in Wonderland
and *Alice Through the Looking Glass*
by Lewis Carroll

FABER & FABER

First published in 2015
by Faber and Faber Ltd
74–77 Great Russell Street
London WC1B 3DA

Typeset by Country Setting, Kingsdown, Kent CT14 8ES
Printed in England by CPI Group (UK) Ltd, Croydon CR0 4YY

A CIP record for this book is available from the British Library

978–0–571–32990–8

2 4 6 8 10 9 7 5 3 1

'Humankind cannot bear very much reality'

T. S. Eliot

wonder.land was commissioned by Manchester International Festival, the National Theatre, London, and the Théâtre du Châtelet, Paris. It was first performed at the Palace Theatre, Manchester, on 2 July 2015. The cast, in alphabetical order, was as follows:

Dum, Ensemble Sam Archer
Aly Lois Chimimba
White Rabbit, Ensemble Rob Compton
Alice Rosalie Craig
Dodo, Ensemble Ivan De Freitas
Keiran, Lizard, Ensemble Luke Fetherston
Cheshire Cat, Caterpillar Hal Fowler
Ms Manxome Anna Francolini
Ensemble Lorraine Graham
Matt Paul Hilton
Kitty, Ensemble Karina Hind
Hedgehog, Ensemble Holly James
Dee, Ensemble Sam Mackay
Mary Ann, Ensemble Daisy Maywood
Luke Enyi Okoronkwo
Mouse, Ensemble David Page
Bianca Golda Rosheuvel
Mock Turtle, Ensemble Cydney Uffindell-Phillips
Dinah, Ensemble Witney White

Director Rufus Norris
Set Designer Rae Smith
Projections 59 Productions
Costume Designer Katrina Lindsay

Lighting Designer Paule Constable
Sound Designer Paul Arditti
Choreographer Javier De Frutos
Music Supervisor David Shrubsole
Associate Director James Bonas
Associate Set Designer Tom Paris
Associate Lighting Designer Rob Casey
Associate Sound Designer Rob Bettle
Puppet Design 'Charlie' Toby Olié

wonder.land, in the version published here, was first performed in London on the Olivier stage of the National Theatre on 23 November 2015. The cast, in order of appearance, was as follows:

M.C. Hal Fowler
Aly Lois Chimimba
Bianca Golda Rosheuvel
Matt Paul Hilton
Dinah Witney White
Kitty Abigail Rose
Mary Ann Stephanie Rojas
Alice Carly Bawden
White Rabbit Joshua Lacey
Ms Manxome Anna Francolini
Luke Enyi Okoronkwo
Mr King Adrian Grove
Dum Sam Archer
Dee Leon Cooke
The Mouse / Keiran Ed Wade
Humpty Daisy Maywood
Dodo Ivan de Freitas
Mock Turtle Cydney Uffindell-Phillips
WPC Rook Nadine Cox
Ensemble / Swing Simon Anthony
Ensemble / Swing Dylan Mason
Ensemble / Swing Lisa Ritchie

Director Rufus Norris
Set Designer Rae Smith
Projections 59 Productions

Lighting Designer Paule Constable
Music Supervisor Tom Deering
Music Associate Malcolm Forbes-Peckham
Sound Designer Paul Arditti
Choreographer Javier De Frutos
Associate Director James Bonas
Associate Set Designer Tom Paris
Associate Choreographer Cydney Uffindell-Phillips
Staff Director Tinuke Craig
Company Voice Work Jeannette Nelson

Characters

The M.C.
Mister Cat, human embodiment
of the Cheshire Cat

Aly
a girl of thirteen

Bianca
her mother, black, thirties (the White Queen)

Matt
her father, white, forty (the Mad Hatter)

Alice
her avatar

The Cheshire Cat, The Caterpillar
both played by the M.C.

The White Rabbit

Ms Manxome
Head Teacher (the Red Queen)

Luke Laprel
a schoolboy (the Knave)

Mr King
a maths teacher

WPC Rook
a police officer

SCHOOLCHILDREN IN THEIR TEENS

Dinah
Kitty
Mary Ann
Kieran

AVATARS

Dum
Dee
Mouse
Humpty
Dodo
Mock Turtle

Customers, waiters, schoolchildren, police,
zombies, playing-card people etc.

Songs

Prologue
Who's Ruining Your Life?
Network
WWW
Fabulous
Falling
I'm Right
Freaks
Crap Life
Who Are You?
Secrets
In Clover
Chances

Me
Heartless Useless
Me (Reprise)
Gadget
Everyone Loves Charlie
O Children
Broken Glass
Fabulous (Reprise)
Who Is Alice?
I'm Right (Reprise)
Secrets (Reprise)
WWW (Reprise)

WONDER.LAND

Act One

PROLOGUE

What sounds like an ordinary stage management announcement begins:

M.C. Good evening, ladies and gentlemen, welcome to tonight's performance in the Olivier Theatre. Please make sure that all mobile phones are turned off – not just on silent mode, but completely off

The M.C. is revealed making the announcement: the human embodiment of the Cheshire Cat. He is playing on a smartphone as she speaks.

May I remind you that filming, texting, tweeting, playing poker, chasing fruit, high-speed racing, zombie slaying, flying through the galaxy and taking selfies during performances – these things are *fabulous* . . .

SONG – PROLOGUE

M.C.
Look at this
In my hands
It obeys
My commands
A digital black portal
To boundless lands

Hours go by
You forget
Night is day
Where's the threat?
Communicate

3

Enter here
Come this way
Swipe the screen
And survey
A world of information and play

Look at this
In my hand
My domain . . .
Here it expands
Until it fills this darkness
With wonderland

The M.C.'s phone rings.

Sorry, I've got to take this
Hello?
Yes? Oh yes . . .

Who are you?
Who am I?
I asked first – Who are *you*?

ONE
LOOKING-GLASS WORLD

The M.C. reveals Aly in her bedroom, a girl of thirteen, playing a game on her smartphone.

SONG – WHO'S RUINING YOUR LIFE?

Aly
I'm moving all the colours
Matching little rows
Green and red and yellow
Redistributing blues
And my score is rising
No clouds on my horizon

4

No thoughts at all in here
Relief from every care
I am marooned in space
Floating like I'm made of air

*Bianca, her harassed mother, comes to the door with
Charlie, aged thirteen months.*

Bianca Alice, what are you doing in there? You've been
in that room all weekend

Aly So?

Bianca
We're going out
So come on, get your hoody on
We're going to the supermarket

Aly
You're joking –

Bianca

Only coaxing

Aly

No!

*Bianca smothers her frustration and collects her
thoughts.*

Bianca
Time
Time is so fleeting
In the hours you're wasting
The daylight is receding

Aly
Why can't you just leave me?

Bianca
Your senses need feeding
I'm pleading, I'm entreating –

Aly

It's just so boring
And I'm having fun

Bianca

How can you sustain your brain?
I can't believe you're entertained

Aly

Oh

Bianca

In this stuffy room
So come on get your hoody on
We're going to the supermarket

Aly

Go on your own

Bianca

                    You can leave the phone

Aly

                                        No

Bianca (*taking Aly's phone, leaving it on her bed*)

Get off your bum

Aly

                Don't wanna come

Bianca

                            Now

I'll blow a fuse, I'm telling you
That armageddon will ensue

Aly reluctantly follows Bianca on to the street. We see the world through her eyes. It is grey and colourless and all the people in it are grey.

Aly

Who's ruining my life?

Chorus

Your mum
Your mum

Aly

Who's ruining my life?

Chorus

Your mum

Aly

Who's ruining my life now?

Chorus

Your mum
Your mum

Aly

Who's ruining your life?

Chorus

Your mum

Aly

She's always on my case
Always at me with some grief
All she does is moan

Bianca

Can you put away the phone?

Aly and Bianca travel on a bus, which is driven by the M.C.

Aly

Even sitting on the bus she's always asking me stuff
Doesn't matter what

Bianca

What homework have you got?
It's usually science at the weekend. Have you done it?

Aly

She's always asking me stuff

Bianca

Have you done it?

Aly

She's always asking me stuff

Bianca

Have you done it?

Aly

She's always asking me stuff

Bianca

Have you done it?

Aly

Who's ruining my life now?

The bus has transported them to the supermarket. Bianca sets off shopping, leaving Aly behind on her own.

Chorus

Your mum
Your mum

Aly

Who's ruining my life?

Chorus

Your mum

Aly

Who's ruining my life now?

Chorus

Your mum
Your mum

Aly

Who's ruining your life?

Aly's dad, Matt, is among the shoppers; wearing several hats and a crumpled suit.

Matt

Hey, look at you, my Alice

Aly Dad . . .

Matt

Lighting up the aisle
Climb into my trolley and

*Aly climbs into Matt's trolley. He starts to spin her
around.*

I'll take you for a spin
Our lucky moon is rising
Clear on our horizon
I'll whirl you through the crowds
As if we were alone in here
And I am the man
Who's always got a better plan

Matt is still spinning Aly around.

Aly

Oh

Matt

Your biggest fan
So come on, take my hand
We're dancing in the supermarket

Aly Dad, can I come and live with you?

*Matt's trolley crashes, causing chaos. Bianca reappears
with Charlie.*

Matt Hello, Bianca

Bianca

Who's ruining your life?

Chorus

Your dad

Matt
  Dodgy trolley; not my fault

Chorus
  Your dad

Aly
  It's not his fault

Bianca
  Who's ruining your life?

Chorus
  Your dad

Bianca I should call the store manager

Matt Is that a threat?

Chorus
  Who's ruining your life now?
  Your dad

Bianca (*to Aly*) You want to live with him?

Chorus
  Your dad

Matt To get away from your moaning

Chorus / Who's ruining your life?

Bianca We'd still be together if it wasn't for your debts

Matt You drove me away

Bianca Those loans were yours. I just paid the price

Aly
  Who's ruining my life?

Chorus
  Your mum

  Matt is trying to help.

Bianca
  Fool

Chorus
  Your dad

Matt
  Nag

Chorus
  Your debts

Bianca
  Twit

Chorus
  Your moans

Aly
  Mum

Chorus
  Your threats

Matt
  Cow

Chorus
  Your loans

Aly
  Dad

Chorus
  Your debts

Bianca
  Fool

Chorus
  Your moans

Aly
  Don't

Chorus
  Your threats

Matt
Nag

Chorus
Your loans

Bianca
Slob

Chorus
Your mum

Matt and Bianca argue over the following chorus:

Your dad, your debts, your moans
Your threats, your loans, your debta
Your moans, your threats your loans
Your dad, your mum

Matt I've been waiting in here all day for a chance of seeing you

Bianca Why? There'd be more chance of seeing us if you put things right

Matt That's what I am doing – (*Pulling a battered cheap bouquet out of his trolley.*) These are for you

Bianca I don't want them!! Why don't you get a job and pay back some of the money you lost? / You ridiculous man

Matt You're like a piece of concrete, you

Aly is rushing home.

Chorus
Who's ruining your life?

Aly Parents!

Aly has made it back to her bedroom. She shuts her door on the whole world.

TWO
DOWN THE RABBIT HOLE

With great relief, Aly picks up her phone.

SONG – NETWORK

Chorus
Let me into your life
Follow trends
Share your everything
Find your friends
Let me into your life
Share your everything

*All over the town, lights are coming on and people on
their own are seeking the network. They include
some owners of the avatars we will later meet.*

Aly
Hello netfriends, is anyone awake?
Hello? Hello, hello, hi?

M.C.
With the net in my life
I am not alone
Share my everything
I can now bring the world to my life
Share my everything

Aly
Saw my dad today
I can't get used to him not being around
I'd like to talk to someone
Message me, I'm here

Bianca (*at her door*)
Aly, are you OK?
You're not alone

I am always here
We can talk
You can let me into your life
I'm always here

Aly

I'm really tired, Mum. I'll probably just go straight
to bed

Bianca (*disappointed*)
OK. Sweet dreams, my love

She exits. Aly is straight back on the network.

Aly

Funny, moving to a new part of town
New flat
Still feeling a bit new at school
Finding my way

*Three of Aly's 'friends' appear: schoolgirls Dinah, Kitty
and Mary Ann.*

Dinah What are you doing on my wall?

Aly You said OK to my Friend Request

Dinah Did I?

Aly I'm Alice – Aly

Dinah Oh Alice, yeah, you're that new girl with the
atmosphere

Aly What atmosphere?

Dinah Like, why d'you never speak?

Aly I do speak. I'm speaking now

Mary Ann Maybe she's got Fat Attitude

Dinah L.O.L.

Kitty I've been reading about that. Fat actually does
something hormonally. It emits something

Dinah giggles.

Aly What are you talking about?

Mary Ann It puts out a chemical that makes thin people think 'Oh no' when they see fat people coming

Dinah laughs.

Aly I'm not fat

Mary Ann No

Kitty But have you thought about stapling it?

Dinah Woi

Aly Seriously, I'm not fat. You must have mixed me up with someone else

Kitty Oh wait a minute; I think I've got a photo. Is that you, there?

She posts an image of Aly, doctored to make her look obese. The girls laugh.
Aly goes under her duvet.

Dinah Has she gone?

Kitty I think so

Dinah Bye-ee

Kitty Sometimes I worry that we're a bit mean

Mary Ann Yeah

Dinah Yeah

Kitty But she's got issues . . .

Dinah Has she?

Kitty Is that why she left her old school?

Mary Ann The family split, isn't it – cos of her dad

Aly (*reappearing*) Shut up

Mary Ann He went bust; lost all their money

Kitty How?

Mary Ann Gambling online

Dinah Is it?

Kitty Is it?

Aly Shut up

Dinah What an idiot

Aly Shut up

Mary Ann I heard he's ill – like not physically

Aly Shut *up*

Kitty He's mental?

Mary Ann You know what I mean? – Like if you look on her wall, there's this photo of him in this dutty old hat

Aly Shut your face

Kitty OMG – Is that him?

Dinah The Mad Hat Man. He's lupoid

They are laughing.

Aly
Shut up you slags
Shut up you slags
Shut up you slags
I hope you die

Aly's words appear on the screen. The girls are outraged. They further deface the picture of Aly.

Girls
So you want in our life?
You think you can
Share our everything?

Kitty
Get a grip

Dinah
Get a life

Mary Ann
Get some popularity

Girls
Be someone else

They disappear. Only the defaced, fat, spotty, melting image of Aly is left. Aly destroys it.

Aly Be someone else

Aly pastes BE SOMEONE ELSE *into her search engine. The wonder.land logo begins to appear – and with it the M.C.*

M.C. Be Someone Else
Take a new direction –
wonder.land

Aly I hate all these games. I hate everything

M.C. Enter your username

Aly I don't wanna enter my username; it's crap

M.C.
wonder.land
No rules here

Aly Is this a virus?

M.C. Come this way

Aly Which way?

M.C. That depends on where you're going

Aly What if I'm going nowhere?

M.C. Then be someone else

   Aly 'enters' AllyPally32.

To create your avatar, press OK

Aly Right, bring it on

   Aly presses OK.

SONG – WWW

During this song, the avatar of Alice is made. She looks just as Aly describes.

M.C.
   www dot wonder.land

Aly
   I'll be a different girl

M.C.
   www dot wonder.land

Aly
   Let's give this crap a whirl

M.C.
   www dot wonder.land

Aly
   As far as I can go from the Alice that I know
   Erase me, go on, chuck me in the waste

M.C.
   So
   Who do you want to be?

Aly
   I have got a notion
   For eyes like the ocean
   See what this golden blonde can be
   Let nothing correspond to me

18

M.C.
 Dot

Aly I'll be a different girl

M.C.
 www dot wonder.land

Aly
 Disguise me
 Let's improvise me

M.C.
 www dot wonder.land

Aly
 Take it on the chin
 I'm going to be thin
 I'm going to look so friendly
 Fight like a frenzy

 I'd like to have some jewels on
 Like diamonds in my hair
 And massive high-heeled shoes on
 So I can walk on air
 As if I never had a single care . . .

M.C.
 www dot wonder.land

Aly
 I'll be a different girl

M.C.
 www dot wonder.land

Aly
 The kind that people like
 Put the bad stuff right
 Make me
 Make me bold and fearless

Little bit of weirdness
I wanna be the real thing
I reckon you can make me sing

As Alice is formed, her eerie, high voice adds to the texture of the song.

This vivid world is
Slowly unfurling
I'll be amazing
My guns are blazing

I'll do what I like now with a wicked sense of fun
I don't need to have a family, I don't need a dad
   and mum
I don't need a little brother and I'll never fall apart
I'm confident and daring cos I've got a brand-new heart

Alice becomes real.

I'll find a place to hide here
And someone new to be
This golden girl I spy here
Is going to be me

M.C. Username AllyPally32. Your avatar is complete

Aly Wow . . . Look at me

M.C. Please agree to our term and condition

Aly There's only one?

M.C. Extreme malice will result in your deletion

Aly Extreme Alice?

M.C. The desire to harm someone; spite, malevolence, ill will

Aly Oh, malice

M.C. Other than that, there are no rules

Aly No rules? (*Pressing OK.*) OK

M.C. Avatar activated

  Alice looks at Aly.

Aly Hello avatar. Right, you're me

Alice You're me

Aly No, you're me

Alice Right, you're me

Aly You're Alice, you dimwit

Alice I'm Alice, you dimwit

Aly No, you're me. I'm not you, right? I'm real

Alice I'm real, not you, right?

Aly You're really fake

Alice No, you're fake

Aly No I'm not

Alice Yes I am

Aly Oh are you?

Alice Yes you are

Aly Whatever, minger. Ain't nobody got time for that

  Alice has copied Aly's actions for these words.

Aly / Alice Brownies' honour
  Put one down
  Do the splits and turn around

  They are both laughing.

Aly OK, Alice, what shall we do?

M.C. To enter the game
You press OK

Aly presses OK. The M.C. and the avatar Cheshire Cat become one.

M.C.
Fabulous
You can be
Fabulous

Aly Sick

As Aly moves, Alice follows her.

Alice Sick

M.C.
Have the whole world at your feet
And be
The person who you really are
Be free

Aly Why are you saying 'Be free?' I am free.

M.C.
That's right
Come closer
Live in a world like this
It's fabulous
Come find your way
It's fabulous

Aly Can I really do what I like?

M.C.
You can be anyone you want
Be free

Aly OK, dance, Alice. I never dance

M.C.
A world of wonder and liberty

Aly Dance better, faster, come on

M.C.
Eat me

Aly Sing

Alice (*singing*)
Pussy cat, pussy cat, pussy cat, pussy cat

Aly Oh my God this is so weird

Alice
Pussy cat, pussy cat, pussy cat, pussy cat

Aly Kick, Alice. Fight. Kick harder

M.C. / Chorus
Have the whole world at your feet
And be
The person who you really are
Be free
Oh press OK

Alice does some amazing high-kicks and fight moves.
She impresses Aly.

Aly Oh that's epic

Alice You're epic

Aly I'm epic

M.C. To game, press the playing card icon
To quest, follow the White Rabbit

Alice Quest or game?

Aly I'm going to quest

Aly presses the White Rabbit icon.

The White Rabbit appears. Like Alice, the White Rabbit can move between the real world and the AV world.

Aly Hey you!

Alice Hey you!

Aly Follow him

The White Rabbit jumps down a rabbit hole.

Jump

And suddenly Alice is falling down the rabbit hole. It is wondrous.

SONG – FALLING

Aly
Curious, curious

Alice
Curious, curious

M.C.
Nothing in wonder.land that you can't do

Aly
This is amazing

Alice
Curious, curious

Aly
This wonderful

M.C.
Nothing in wonder.land that you can't do

Aly
This is amazing

Alice
Curious, curious

Aly
This wonderful

M.C.
Nothing in wonder.land that you can't do

Aly
There's nothing that I can't do

Aly
I'm falling

Aly / Alice
I'm falling down
Down underground

Aly
I'll never

Alice
Never be found

Bianca's voice joins, as if waking Aly from a dream.

Bianca Aly, Aly?

THREE
THE MANXOME FOE

*Bianca helps Aly dress for school. As Aly plays, the
White Rabbit runs through the space.*

Bianca Aly? Did you not hear me call? You'll be late for
school! I would have woken you earlier but Charlie
threw up on my shoes. He really is King Puke – and his
nappy's full. I don't know how he does so much. I'll miss
my train again. I've taken some drumsticks out of the
freezer. When you get home put them in the oven with
some wedges

Aly Yeah

Bianca There's a wash on. Can you stick it in the dryer and put the big stuff on the rack?

Aly Yeah

Bianca There's a whole pile of babygrows that need folding and putting away

Aly Yeah

Bianca And feed the Venus Fly Trap. I'll be back from the child-minder at six – Do you need your PE kit?

Aly Yeah

Bianca Will you brush your teeth?

Aly Yeah

Bianca Have you got your homework?

Aly Yeah

Bianca Will you pack your lunch?

Aly Yeah

Bianca Take some fruit

Aly Yeah

Bianca What's the fifth element of the periodic table?

Aly Yeah

Bianca It's boron – yeah

Bianca has finally got Aly's attention. She turns to go.

Aly Mum?

Bianca turns back, hoping for some communication.

Bianca Yes, love?

Aly You got your skirt tucked in your tights

Bianca Don't play on that phone at school, OK?

The school bell goes. The White Rabbit continues to lead the chase.

Aly (*into her phone*) Come on, Alice, keep up with him. There!

Aly finds herself in the school playground. Other children are eyeing her curiously.

That rabbit's on crack or something

Aly is oblivious to:

Ms Manxome I'll have that

She looks round in terror as her Head Teacher, Ms Manxome, takes her phone.

Thank you, my dear. It seems you children need reminding

The children scramble into assembly. Ms Manxome holds Aly's phone aloft.

SONG – I'M RIGHT

Ms Manxome
These phones are banned,
If I discover one in your hand, it's mine
You've lost it now
And I'll tell you again
That they drive me insane –
They're banned

Aly Sorry, Miss, I didn't know

Ms Manxome
Ignorance is no excuse here
Come plead at break
There is no need to quake
What's the matter? don't shake
I'm no venomous snake
But make no mistake
I'm right

Sit.

Aly sits

I'm right, I'm right, I'm right in every single thing I do
That's why I'm held in esteem, why my trophies
    all gleam, why my school is supreme, I'm right

Tell her, children

Chorus
    She's right, she's right, she's right in every single thing
      she does

Ms Manxome
    I'm never wrong; other teachers all throng when I'm
      banging my gong for I've never been, ever been wrong

Luke Laprel walks in late, trying not to be noticed.

Luke Laprel

Luke Yes, Miss?

Ms Manxome
    Lovely, likeable Luke.
    Lamentably, lethally late

Luke Sorry, Miss

Ms Manxome
    O children
    When will you realise that this is all for you?
    I'll express it in a medium that you regard as true

She calls.
    *Mr King enters with a huge 1990s beat box on his
shoulder.*

Ms Manxome Press the thing

*Mr King presses 'play'. The machine launches into a
rap beat. Mr King joins in on occasional line endings.*

A year ago
This school was down
Worst on the block

Worst in the town
Your head teacher was gone
Moved on
Whereupon
I arrived in his stead
My knowledge to spread
I'm ploughing ahead
So your brain will be fed
I'm your special measure
Educational treasure
A government czar
Take a ride in my car
I've got your 'A' star
You'll go far.
I'm your warrior queen
Teaching's my scene
I'm not your jailer
But I make war on failure
Mess me about?
You're out
I'm your saviour
From bad behaviour
Try my edifying flavour
Nose to the grindstone
This is the mind zone
Step out of line
And I'm dread.
No cheek, no phones,
Take your weird artwork home.
My battlecry echoes
All over your ghettoes
Improve my school
Revere my rule
Hear what I said
Or it's off with your head!

Mr King Boom

He turns off the beat box.

Ms Manxome I love you kids

The bell goes. As the children disperse to their classes:

Ms Manxome
I'm right

Chorus
She's right

Ms Manxome
I'm right

Chorus
She's right

Ms Manxome
I'm right in every single thing

Chorus
Single thing

Ms Manxome
I do

Chorus
She does

Ms Manxome Stand

Chorus
She's never wrong

Ms Manxome That's right

Chorus
Other teachers all throng when she's banging her gong
for she's never been, ever been, never been, ever been,
never been, ever been, never been, ever been wrong

*Ms Manxome is now alone in her office. She drops her
public face.*

Ms Manxome
  Another day enforcing order
  I cannot bemoan the fact I'm alone
  And that sometimes I'm prone
  To a vague undertone of dejection –
  An interior groan that I always disown
  For my duty is sewn into my marrow bone.
  It is hewn on the front of my
  Lonely tombstone

  She slices the head off one of her flowers with her
  guillotine. Aly has appeared at the door and is
  watching her.

Aly You said to come and plead, Miss

  Ms Manxome looks round, startled.

About my phone

Ms Manxome Ah yes. You're the new girl, aren't you?
From the broken home. Remind me of your name?

Aly Alice Hatton

Ms Manxome Alice . . . do you know what your name
means?

Aly No

Ms Manxome It means noble, of the nobility. It's my
name too. Alice Manxome

Aly Oh

  Ms Manxome returns Aly's phone.

Ms Manxome I'm sure we'll be great friends. But Alice,
if I find you with this phone again, it's a beheading – I
mean a detention

  Aly leaves, chastened.

My wisdom I've shared,
I've pastorally cared
Even though she's impaired
That girl is prepared
For her future; she's saved
She'll turn out well behaved
Because I am right

FOUR
THE POOL OF TEARS

Aly and her classmates are lining up outside a classroom.
Dinah, Mary Ann and Kitty surround Aly.

Dinah Alice?

Aly Hi

Mary Ann Hi

Kitty Hi

Dinah I've been feeling a bit mean. It must be tough
starting a new school

Kitty We've all been feeling a bit mean

Mary Ann That picture we put up was nasty

Dinah And all that stuff you said about us being slags?

Kitty We think we were a bit slaggy

Aly I didn't mean it. I'd never usually say anything like
that

Dinah I think it's not too late to start again

Aly Really?

Dinah So what about that Friend Request?

Aly You want to be friends?

Mary Ann Sure we do

Aly Oh . . . that's great

Dinah All you have to do say is sorry

Mary Ann For wishing we were dead

Aly Yeah, I don't know what came over me. I'm really sorry. There's no way I wish you were dead

Dinah You just have to say 'Please forgive me, Dinah'

Kitty Say 'I'm so stupid'

Mary Ann Say 'I'm just a big fat bitch'

The bell rings.
Dinah addresses the rest of the class.

Dinah Guys, Alice has been bullying us online

Aly What?

Kitty She's a real troll

Aly No I'm not

Mary Ann She actually put a death-wish on us, can you believe it?

Kitty She wants us all dead

Mary Ann It's on her wall

Dinah She sits in her bedroom and ruins people's lives

Mr King enters. He starts writing on a whiteboard.

Mr King Right, you lot, worksheets out. Today, we're going to be looking at surds. Now a surd is a square root that cannot be reduced to a rational number. For example –

Luke enters, late.

Mr King Luke Laprel what is a surd?

Luke I think our cat did one this morning, sir.

Mr King Final warning.

The girls whispers harshly to Aly.

Mary Ann BIG

Kitty FAT

Dinah BITCH

Aly gets her phone out under the desk.

M.C. Welcome, AllyPally32

Aly I'm in wonder.land

Alice enters, following the White Rabbit. The classroom becomes the hall of doors.

Alice, stop

Alice But I have to follow the White Rabbit

Aly Shut up. Cry

Alice cries. The White Rabbit stops running and regards her.

(*To the White Rabbit.*) Stop. What are you looking at?

Alice Get lost, Big Ears

The White Rabbit is taken aback. He goes.

Aly (*to Alice*) Cry more

Alice cries harder.

Nobody likes you
No wonder you haven't got any friends

Alice Nobody likes me

Aly Everything's your fault

Aly Cry harder, you big fat bitch

Alice It's all my fault

Aly Cry a pool

Alice I'm so lonely

Aly Cry a whole pool of tears and then throw yourself in

Alice's crying reaches new heights.
  Dum and Dee, incredibly fat twins, enter fighting.

Dum I saw it

Dee Well, it's gone

Dum It was here

Dee Who cares about a garden anyway?

Dum You chose this stupid game

Dee You chose it

Dum No I didn't

Dee Are you calling me a liar?

Dum I'm calling you a freak

SONG – FREAKS

Dee
  You've led us down this wormhole

Dum
  It's your fault that we're sunk

Dee
  At least I'm not as dumb as you

Dum
  You're worse, you piece of junk

Alice Who are they?

Dum / Dee (*ignoring her*)
  Freak

Dee
  Loser

Dum
  Creep

Dee
  Freak

Dum
  You make me throw up

Dee
  Why don't you grow up?

Aly They must be other players

Dum	**Dee**
Pig	Dog
Dum	**Dee**
Slob	Slag
Dum	**Dee**
Butters	Hag

Dum
  Hog

Dee	**Dum**
Crap ballerina	What a hyena

They fight.

Aly Greet them

Dee
  You smell like kangaroo poo

Dum
  You've got iguana breath

Dee
Is that the best that you can do?

Dum   **Dee**
I hate you   Living death

Alice (*tentatively*)
Hi, hello freaks, hi
Maybe you ought to
Be a bit nicer

Aly
Alice, you've got to be cooler –

Alice (*cooler*)
Hey, freakish big guys, yo
Pause with the slaughter

Dum Who d'you think you are, Paedo?

Aly Woi

Dum and Dee turn on Alice.

Dum
I bet that you're a dogface
Your avatar's so cute

Dee
Yeah, you only made her
Cos you're fugly as a boot

Aly / Alice (*outraged*) What did you say?

Dee   **Dum**
Freak   Dog

Aly Now wait a minute

Dee   **Dum**
Minger   Slob

Dee   **Dum**
Geek   Crutters

37

Dum / Dee
Dressing up so sweet

Aly No I don't

Dum / Dee
Bet you're a sad freak

Alice / Aly
Listen, losers –
I don't like the way you're talking

Dee	**Dum**
Mank	Minger

Dee	**Dum**
Munter	Mare

Dee	**Dum**
Butters	Rank

Alice
Don't you dare

Dum / Dee
Face made of concrete

Aly OK, that's enough

Alice / Aly
I hope you're feeling wary
Cos you're asking for it now

Dum
You're such a scary mary

Dee	**Dum**
Call for Mummy	Have a cow

Aly Alice, stick up for yourself

Alice fights Dum and Dee.

Dum Stop

Dee No don't hurt us

Dum We're nice

Dee Stop or we'll cry

Dum (*to Dee*) Cry

  Dee cries. Dum cries.

Aly Unbelievable

Dum You made us cry

Alice Why did you insult me like that?

Dum You insulted us

Dee You insulted two poor little helpless –

Dum Fat guys

Dee Yeah, two helpless big fat guys

Alice Are you twins?

Dum Of course we're twins

Aly / Alice Are you girls?

Dum No

Dee Yes

Dum No

Dee No

Dum No

Dee Yes

Dum No

Dee Yes

  *Other avatars have approached: The Mouse, who is
  vast, and Humpty, who is a pale ghost-like child
  holding a large balloon.*

Mouse Hey, Blondie

Aly / Alice Ahhhh!

Alice What are you?

Mouse I'm a giant, terrifying mouse. Actually, the mouse is just a shell, hiding one hundred per cent dench

Alice I'm Alice

Aly Don't tell him your name

Alice I'm not Alice

Aly Yes I am but

Alice Yes I am

Mouse Are you confused? Because I can put you right

Aly Wrong

Mouse Have you worked out what we're supposed to do in this game?

Aly No

Dum Yes

Dee No

Dum Yes

Dee Yes

Alice No

Mouse I was watching you fight these fat creeps; not bad – for a girl

Alice What makes you think I'm a girl?

Humpty You were crying

Aly No I wasn't

Humpty Yes, you cried a whole pool

Aly / Alice What's with the balloon?

Humpty It's not a balloon, it's my head. Were you going to swim?

Alice What?

Humpty In your tears?

Aly (*irritated*) I don't know

The Dodo enters: a muscled birdman. He strikes a pose.

Dodo Hi (*He abandons the pose.*) Have you seen the garden?

Humpty Yeah

Dum We saw it

Dee No we didn't

Dum Yes we did

Aly / Alice What garden?

Dodo It appears – and every time I think I'm getting close, it gets further away

Alice Why are you dressed as a duck?

Dodo I'm a dodo. I feel pretty close to extinction most of the time

Mock Turtle Me too

There is a bin nearby. It is an avatar: the Mock Turtle.

Alice Have you been there all along?

Mock Turtle Yes

Alice What are you?

Mock Turtle I'm a mock turtle

Aly Let's have a look

Mock Turtle I can't show you

Alice Why not?

Mock Turtle I went wrong. I made such a crap avatar that I just trashed it

Aly Say something kind

Alice Your bin's nice

Mock Turtle Yeah, I really like it in the bin

Humpty So what brought you here?

Mouse Hormones

Dodo I'm taking time off from my course of study actually. I'm under huge pressure to stop the planet from dying

Alice Really?

Dodo My parents say it's all up to me. I think their expectations are unrealistic

Humpty My parents don't have any expectations

Dee We're under huge pressure

Dum That's what it's like when you're a dancer

Dee You're under huge pressure

Dum We're growing too big

Mouse You got big jubblies?

Dum No

Mouse King-size baps, is that what you're saying?

Dee No

Mouse Giant jelly melons?

Alice / Aly What is your problem?

Mouse Sorry, am I being a dick?

Everyone Yes

Mouse Every time I go in a new game, I think 'This time I won't be a dick.' And then I'm a dick. Have you got big jugs though?

Dee You don't understand what it's like

Dum Big dancers are losers

Dee We need to be tiny and thin

Humpty So, Alice, what about you?

Alice What about me?

Mouse What size are yours?

Humpty I mean, what's going on for you?

Dodo Who are you?

Alice I'm a big fat bitch

Aly No I'm not

Alice Yes I am

Aly Alice

Alice You said so

Aly No I didn't

Alice You absolutely did

Aly OK, fine

Aly / Alice I am a big fat birtch

Humpty So's my mum

Humpty
Sometimes I hear my stepdad shouting
Piss off to bed
Or I'll give you a clouting

Dodo
I think that I'm twisted
In the head

Mock Turtle
They call me Pizza Face at school

Mouse
I'm really small
Girls find me really boring

All
Where is this wonderland
Where I can be me?

Mock Turtle
I never like to leave my bedroom
Panic attacks

Dum / Dee
We're thin as tennis rackets

Humpty
My mum's never sober

Mouse
I'm a prat

Dodo
Sometimes I wear my sister's bra
Why is that wrong?

Aly / Alice
I feel like I'm belonging

All
Where is this wonderland
Where I can be me?

Humpty
Smoking fags
Drinking dregs
Longing for the day when I can pack my bags

Aly / Alice
Oh
It's a crap life

Mock Turtle
Look obscene
Need a cream
Face like something out of Halloween

All
Oh
It's a crap life

Dum *and* **Dee**
Got no friends
'Cept my twin
And the contents of a biscuit tin

All
Oh
It's a crap life

Aly / Alice
Feel a little bit lonely
Like a mouldy cherry left there rotting in the bowl

All
Oh, oh, oh, oh, oh
It's a crap life

Mouse

I haven't grown
Not at all
I haven't even got a hairy ball

All

Oh
It's a crap life

Dodo

Arctic melts
Seas rise
Frocks on cos we're all going to die

The White Rabbit runs through the space, turning it into a beautiful garden; light, colourful, magnificent.

All

Oh
It's a crap life
Wonderland
Place to hide
Armageddon going on outside
Oh
It's a crap life
Feel a little bit lonely
Found a place I want to spend a little bit of time
Oh
It's a crap life

Aly's involvement in the scene has taken her to her feet.

Mr King Alice Hatton? What are you doing on your feet?

Mr King and the classroom reanimate. Alice, the avatars and wonder.land disappear.

Aly I was just . . .

Kitty She's sleepwalking, sir

Mary Ann She's wetting herself, sir

Dinah She's got mental problems, sir

Mr King (*to Aly*) Answer that question

Aly Um. Two

Mr King Have you been listening to anything I've said?

Aly Sorry, sir

The bell goes.

Mr King Alice Hatton, you're on a warning. Finish the worksheet. And I want five hundred words on why surds are fun.

Mr King goes. The three girls surround Aly like witnesses.

Dinah So what's it going to be, Alice?

Kitty Do you still want to be friends?

Mary Ann Are you ready to say sorry?

Dinah Then you can be our bitch

Aly What is your problem?

Dinah My problem? I don't have a problem

Aly Yes you do; what is it? Why are taking it out on me?

Dinah Because you get right up my nose

Aly You got nose hair? Cos I've heard too much body hair can be really scarring. Have you got a little moustache as well?

Mary Ann (*whispers to Kitty*) How did she know?

Dinah (*to Mary Ann*) Shuup!

Aly You should try a cream, or maybe waxing?

Dinah (*moving in on Aly*) Come here, Fatchops!

Aly runs. Dinah, Mary Ann and Kitty chase her. Alice chases the White Rabbit. Into:

FIVE
ADVICE FROM A CATERPILLAR

Aly enters the girls' toilets and shuts herself in a cubicle.

Aly Alice

Alice Where are we?

Aly Somewhere we can hide

Alice Why can't we be with our friends?

Aly I just want to be with you

The White Rabbit has led Alice into the undergrowth. Everything looks enormous.

And him. I don't mind being with him.

Alice Why do we have to hide?

Aly Because there are monsters out there

We hear the Caterpillar.

Weird

The Caterpillar enters, huge and green, made up of several dancers, including the M.C., smoking an umbrella.

Alice Is that a monster?

Aly I don't know

Alice Ask it

Aly You ask it

Alice Who are you?

Caterpillar Who are *you*?

Alice I asked first; who are you?

Caterpillar The question you need is Who Are You?

Aly Tell him he can see perfectly well who you are

Alice You can see perfectly well who I am

Caterpillar But that's not true, is it? These outer shells are only versions of ourselves. Mine will soon harden and cocoon me quite

Aly Are you another player?

Caterpillar I am the Caterpillar

SONG – WHO ARE YOU?

Who are you?
Who are you?
That's a question true
It's a mystery
For your whole
Life through
Who are you?
Each day
Please ask
Who's behind
Your mask
Who are you?
Who are you?
Who are you?
As a grub
I grew
As I ate
Not a clue
Not a clue

                    As to who
                        I was
                            But the
                                Question runs
                                    Through years
                                    And suns
                                        Through the sands
                                        Of time
                                        Ever round
                                        Your mind
                                    Because
                                    If you don't know
                                Who's
                            At the core
                        Of you
                    You're easy prey
                Or a simple fool
            So it's clear
                That you'll
                    Hear me say
                        Who are you?
                            That's a question
                                True
                                    It's a mystery
                                        For your whole
                                        Life through
                                        Who are you?
                                    Each day
                                    Please ask
                                    Who's behind
                                Your mask
                            Who are you?
                        Who are
            You?

    The Caterpillar smokes.

Alice What shall I tell him?

Aly I don't know

Alice I don't know who I am

Caterpillar Then you will never progress. One day I will transform into a creature of exquisite beauty. I will spread my magnificent wings and fly away – So must *you*. I have some advice

Alice What is it?

Caterpillar Who are *you*?

Aly / Alice That's not advice

Caterpillar It's the only question that matters

The Caterpillar departs.

Each day
   Please ask
      Who's behind
       The mask
      Who are you?
     Who are
  You?

He vanishes.
   Aly becomes aware that the three girls are surrounding her, watching her.

Dinah Hi Aly

Kitty Hi

Mary Ann Hi, you talking to yourself?

Kitty That's a sign of madness

Dinah But then, that runs in your family, doesn't it

Aly Have you come in for a shave?

Dinah Oh that's funny

Aly makes to exit. Kitty and Mary Ann block her.

Mary Ann That is jokes

Aly shuts herself in a cubicle.

Dinah You are hysterical

Kitty She's out of control, isn't she?

They are taking photos of her over the cubicle door.

Aly Why don't you all just eff-off?

Mary Ann / Ohhh

Kitty That was almost the eff-word

Mary Ann That was almost bold

Dinah It's all right, Aly. We understand why you're like this

Mary Ann Yeah, you can't help it, can you?

Kitty It's genetic

Dinah We did a little search about your dad

Kitty Local news site

Dinah He's properly nuts

Mary Ann Backslash mad dad

Aly You are so stupid

Dinah Six months ago he was out on the street, wasn't he? Fighting the debt collectors in his pants

Aly You don't know anything about it

Dinah Is that why your mum left him?

Kitty I mean Hashtag Loser

Mary Ann howls like a loopy wolf.
  Aly comes out of the cubicle.

Aly Why don't you mind your own damn business?

Kitty We're just concerned, Alice

Dinah Yeah - people should know if he's mental

Aly Shut up

  Aly lashes out at Dinah. The girls hurt her

Dinah I do not have facial hair. I am perfect. Say it

Aly I am perfect

  Dinah gives her more pain.

Dinah Your family's a freak show. And if you ever come on my wall again, I'll post that you do sex acts

Mary Ann You do sex acts free in that toilet

  They exit. Aly gets her phone out. Alice appears.

Alice (*singing*) 'Who are you? Who are you? It's a question true . . .' Who are you?

  Aly just shakes her head.

Aly Alice, you don't want to know

Alice Yes I do

Aly I'm really bad

Alice Am I?

Aly I'm really stupid. I'm horrible

Alice Why?

Aly I can't say

Alice Why not?

Aly Cos it's none of your business

Alice Is it a secret?

Aly No

Alice Then say it, Alice. Say it

Aly No

Alice Say it. You can say anything to me

Aly No I can't

Alice You're only saying it to yourself

SONG – SECRETS

Aly
It's possible I've got some secrets
Things I don't want to say

Alice
Is it someone I love,
Or someone I hate,
Or a trust that I cannot betray?

Aly
I've got secrets that loom in my head when I sleep
Secrets I push away somewhere deep

Alice
But once the mouth opens
The words start to come
In a great rush of freedom
The river will run

I'll loyally keep all our secrets
You can tell me without any shame –

Aly
It was my fault, you know
That my dad had to go
Our family broke; I'm to blame

One night, after midnight, I crept down the stairs
There on the sofa sat Dad, in despair

I found out that he had a secret
Each night he was gambling away
His game was roulette
And he'd fallen in debt
He was desperately trying to pay
At first he'd been lucky, but then how he lost
Not just a game cos it came at real cost

Alice

And now the mouth opens
The words start to come

Aly / Alice

A great rush of freedom
The river will run

Aly

Dad begged me to keep it a secret;
I promised I wouldn't tell Mum
But the money ran dry
And when Mum wondered why
I revealed to her all that he'd done.
I broke up their marriage, broke my dad's heart –
It's my fault it all fell apart

It's not my only secret. It's not even my worst

Alice

Say it, Alice
Say it, Alice
Say it, Alice
Say it, Alice

Both

And when the mouth opens
The words start to come
In a great rush of freedom –

Aly I hate being me
I hate it
I totally utterly hate
Being me

Alice Is that my secret?

Aly I wish I was you.

Alice You are me

Aly No I'm not. Everyone likes you. You're not afraid of anything. And you're beautiful

Alice But I hate it

Aly What?

Alice Being me

Aly is taken aback.

And now the mouth opens
The words start to come

Both
In a great rush of freedom
The river will run
The river will run

The White Rabbit appears.

Alice Hey, you

Aly It's the Crack Rabbit

Alice Hi, Big Ears

Aly Am I supposed to follow you again?

The White Rabbit nods.

Aly / Alice Supposing I don't want to?

Alice Supposing I just want to stay here

Aly Would you stay with me?

The White Rabbit considers.

You could tame him, Alice

Alice I could tame you

The White Rabbit shakes his head.

Alice Are you wild?

Aly Don't ask him that

Alice Why not?

Aly It's embarrassing

Alice Why?

Aly Cos he's – I mean I know he's just a computer graphic and everything, but

Alice You're cute

Aly Alice, shuup

Alice He doesn't mind

Aly God-duh

The White Rabbit moves away.

Follow him

And Alice starts to run. She exits after the Rabbit. Suddenly, a boy comes into the toilets, breathless: Luke Laprel.

Luke Need to hide

Aly This is the girls'

Luke So?

Aly Get out

Luke The bell's gone; you get out

Luke is clearly afraid. He positions himself behind the door.

Aly What are you doing here?

Another boy kicks the door open: Kieran Snipe, older, meaner.

What the heck? This is the girls'!

Kieran Did Luke Laprel come in here?

Aly No

Kieran Yes he did, that little piss streak. I just saw him

Aly There's no one here – get out!

Kieran You're hiding that gayboy in here

Aly You are not allowed in our toilets

Kieran Luke Laprel, I am on your case!!

Aly And I'm on yours

Kieran Is that a threat, fat girl?

Aly (*filming him with her phone*) Oh look, a pervert

Kieran What?

Aly Caught in the girls' toilets

Kieran (*backing away*) What are you saying to me?

Aly Oh no, he's so creepy and scary. Will you look under the door while I'm having a wee?

Kieran You better watch it, walrus

Aly Or have you just run out of tampons?

Kieran Urrgh

Aly Get out now, or I'll put this online

Kieran (*backing out*) I'll get you after school, Laprel, you gayer!

Kieran leaves, intimidated. Luke looks at Aly. Aly looks at Luke.

Aly Are you gay?

Luke Are you fat?

The school bell goes.

Aly Aren't you going to class?

Luke Aren't you?

Aly I will if you will

Luke I won't if you won't

Aly doesn't move. Luke and Aly get their smartphones out of their pockets. Luke sits on the floor, absorbed with his game. Aly joins him. They play.

Aly So why does he want to beat you up so badly?

Luke He's a coward. And a hypocrite. He hates me cos he likes me

Aly is intrigued.

Thanks, by the way

Aly No worries. Dealing with other people's bullies is fine. It's just dealing with your own, isn't it?

Luke What are you playing?

Aly Wonder.land

Luke (*looking at her screen*) That your avatar?

Aly Yeah: Alice

Luke She's white

Aly So?

Luke So she's white

Aly My dad's white; why shouldn't she be white?

Luke She's a little white princessy thing

Aly No she's not! I just wanted her to be as far away from me as possible. But she is me

Luke Strange though. People usually make avatars who are cooler than they are. You are definitely cooler than her. And better looking

Aly Are you flirting?

Luke No

Aly Just checking

Luke Just saying

The door bursts open and Ms Manxome comes in. Aly and Luke leap to their feet.
Luke shoves his smartphone in his pocket – but Aly fails to hide hers in time.

Ms Manxome Lurking during lesson time – in the *girls'* toilets?!

Luke The tragedy is that I'm short-sighted, Miss; I went through the wrong door and then I couldn't find my way out

Ms Manxome Detention, both of you. (*She turns to Aly.*) Show me what's behind your back

Aly Nothing, Miss

Ms Manxome You ludicrous dissembler; I can see it in the mirror

Aly Miss, please – I have it in class. It's a learning aid – for my dyslexia

Ms Manxome takes Aly's phone.

Ms Manxome In my day, no one had dyslexia. They had a condition called Thick

Luke You can't say that, Miss; that's child-abuse

Ms Manxome Lackadaisical laughable Luke. Let's hope your fate is not that of the lawless, lysergic, lobotomised loser

Luke Thank you, Miss

Ms Manxome *(to Aly)* Alice Hatton . . .

Aly Miss, honestly, it's like my spellcheck and everything

Ms Manxome Then let's see, shall we? If your browsing history shows nothing but learning aids, you can keep it

She looks at Aly's screen.

Wonder.land? What a funny white bunny; isn't he cute? You can have this back when it's obsolete. Now GO!

Aly and Luke both run.

I should be running the country; not just a school

Alice Alice?

Ms Manxome Who's calling my name?

Alice Where are you?

Ms Manxome If there is anyone else hiding in these toilets I will flush you out

Alice Come on, you big fat bitch

Ms Manxome What?

Alice is laughing. Ms Manxome looks at the phone.

Ms Manxome Oh – how curious. She hasn't locked the screen

Alice Look, we're in the garden; can we try to find our friends?

Ms Manxome No security. This child's an open book

Alice I'm not an open book. I'm keeping your secrets safe, in here (*She presses her heart.*)

Ms Manxome My secrets?

Alice *My* secrets. And I don't have to hide. I'm not afraid of anything

Ms Manxome Of course I'm not

Alice I feel a little bit lonely, but –

Ms Manxome I'm not lonely . . . Who told you I was lonely?

Alice You did

Ms Manxome I know they shun me in the staffroom but –

Alice I don't hate myself

Ms Manxome Of course I don't. I love myself

Alice I love myself

Ms Manxome You look just like I did when I was a child

Alice I am you, you mouldy cherry

Ms Manxome You're me

Alice I love you, Alice

Ms Manxome It's been years and years since anyone said that to me

Alice What would you like me to do?

Ms Manxome What would you like to do?

Alice We've made it to the garden

Ms Manxome Oh, goody

Alice Shall we see what's here?

Ms Manxome Are we allowed?

Alice There are no rules here. We can do whatever we like

SIX
A MAD TEA PARTY

Aly and Luke run into the school playground.

Aly She's got my phone – I cannot survive

Luke She is right out of order

Aly I feel like I lost my hand. That phone is part of me. How can I live without my game?

Luke Yeah, it's pretty harsh

Aly It can't be happening. What can I do? I need to be with Alice!

She realises she has Luke by the lapels.

Sorry

Luke So what's the game?

Aly I'm on a quest

Luke What for?

Aly I don't know

Luke You don't know what your quest is?

Aly No, I think the point of the quest is to find out what the quest is for

Luke That is so girl . . .

63

Aly So what do you play?

Luke Check it out

He hands Aly his smartphone. Zombies appear in the playground all around them.

Zombie Swarm

Aly That is so boy

Luke The only thing that enrages them is when they see a living person. So don't make any sudden movements – or they'll swarm

Aly What happens when they swarm?

Luke They start appearing from everywhere. And all they're concerned about is eating your brain

Aly You should come to wonder.land; seriously

Luke OK

Aly (*surprised*) You want to game with me?

Luke Yeah, my username's Jack Roadkill

Aly is delighted – then remembers her agony:

Aly Mine's AllyPally32. But what can I play on? That teacher took my phone!

The bell goes for the end of day.
Matt is at the school gates, wearing his hat; exuberant.

Matt Aly, you dazzle me

Aly (*dumbfounded*) It's my dad . . .

Matt I could reach right in and take out my heart

Aly Dad, my phone's been confiscated. The Head Teacher took it

Matt So, she's an idiot

Aly But my phone, Dad; what am I going to do?

Matt Come on my darling, forget your problems

Aly Can I borrow yours?

Matt Sure

Matt pulls something out of his pocket that is not a phone.

Aly What is that?

Matt Got rid of my phone. I am technology free. And you're going to come out with me and celebrate

Aly I can't. I've got detention

Matt That's an invention of henchmen
It's not worth a mention
Is this your boyfriend?

Luke / Aly No

Matt Bring him

Luke OK

Aly Are you going to miss your detention?

Luke I will if you will

They leave the school grounds.

SONG – IN CLOVER

Matt
It's time we woke this town up
And showed this place
That we're alive
It's time to tear our frowns up
And realise
We have survived

Chorus
    And realise
    We have survived

Matt
    And so my darling Alice
    I've come to take
    You out to tea
    I've thrown out all my hardware
    And I've found
    Stability

    No more a virtual half-life
    No more of programming I'll hear
    For now I live in clover
    I've gone and got
    A new career

Aly Really?

Chorus
    He's gone and got
    A new career

Aly Dad, seriously? You got a job?

Aly
    You are a man of knowledge

Matt
    Don't underes-
    Timate my skill
    Now, in the garden centre
    The soil
    I'm going to till

Aly Dad, that's great

Matt
    I'm living in the real world
    There'll be no
    More screens for me

Aly
You're going to be so steady
In this harsh
Reality

Chorus
In this harsh
Reality

Aly
You'll have colleagues and a workplace

Matt
They'll hold me tightly
Like a kite

Aly
And pull you gently earthwards

Matt
When I'm at risk
Of mental flight

Chorus
When he's at risk
Of mental flight

Aly Well, I'm proud of you

Matt
I am a child of fortune
I've had my share
Of wretched luck
But now I live in clover
And overflowing
Is my cup

Chorus
And overflowing
Is his cup

Matt is leading Aly and Luke to 'Treacle Teas'. The Waiters hand them menus.

Matt Your best table, please. And a big pot of hot stewing tea

Luke So what did you do before?

Aly He was a programmer, a brilliant one

Matt But it wasn't healthy. It led to some bad habits – which I shall now rectify with the best cakes on the premises

Matt starts playing the spoons.

So how long have you two been in love?

Aly Will you stop embarrassing me?

Matt That's what dads are for, isn't it? (*To Luke.*) Don't get my daughter pregnant, will you?

Luke We're just friends

The Waiters arrive with cakes.

Matt You see, you say that, but then you'll develop facial hair – and the day will come when you realise Aly's radiance and then

Luke I don't think so

Matt Do you not think my daughter is radiant?

Luke I do obviously – but I'm gay

The Waiters all look at Luke.

Matt Seriously?

Luke Yup

Matt And you admit it, just like that?

Luke To you, yeah. Cos you're kind of unthreatening

Matt Oh, I'm a dangerous man, as Aly will tell you

Aly You just get a bit hyper sometimes. Got to remember to calm down

Matt (*to Luke*) I bet you take some shit for that?

Luke A bit

Matt But you know who you are and that's a great thing; that's an amazing thing and you've got to hold on to that. (*He piles the cakes on top of each other.*) You deserve an award cos you are going to have to take your chances, son

Luke I know

Aly Dad, don't do that

Matt You're going to have to play the game – but be yourself. You know what I suggest?

Luke What?

Matt Let us eat cake and raise our cracked teacups to life's chances

SONG – CHANCES

Matt
Sooner or later
You'll begin to see
Life's not for gambling
And your chances are never free
You must grab each passing moment
Each opportunity

Luke Too right

Aly Don't sing

Matt
It's hardly odd that sometimes
We're captured in life's traps
The whole thing is so puzzling
No wonder we collapse
Let's dance through each disaster

Make adversity a song
And build our towers on the sand
To help the tide along

Waiter Excuse me, sir

Matt
Sooner or later
I've begun to see
Life is not a gambling site
And chances don't come free
Clubs are things you're hit with
Diamonds, what you spend
Hearts are pain and happiness
And spades, they dig you
Oh they dig you to your end

A few customers join in.

Customers
To the end

Aly Dad, people are looking

Luke joins in:

Matt / Luke
We're clusters
Mere fragments
We're made of broken glass

Matt
And when we sit upon the shards
They scratch us on the / arm

Aly Dad!

Matt
I feel most uncertain
When thinking of my name
Am I the same as yesterday
Or is it all a game?

Aly (*explaining to the Waiters*)
Sooner or later
His mood will turn around
He gets this wild euphoria
And then he
Then he comes back down

Matt is making friends with the other customers.

Waiter Would you keep the noise down?

*Matt and Luke take over the restaurant, Aly powerless
to stop them.*

Matt
It's hardly odd that sometimes
We're found sitting here like freaks
When we can't take it lying down
Or turn the other cheek
It's time to cash in all our chips
To hang up our balloons
To stave off the apocalypse
By playing on the spoons

Over a spoon chorus:

Aly
Why must I always
Be looking after you?
I really wish I had a dad
Who I could look up to

The Waiters advance on Matt. Aly leaps to his defence.

Waiter
He's bonkers, he's crazy   **Aly**
He's clearly up the creek   Leave him alone!
He's going to spoil our lovely cakes
Let's throw him   **Aly**
                                   That's assault!
Let's throw him in the street   Call the police!

71

Aly pushes the Waiter, hard. A crap scuffle: the Waiter hits Matt. Matt retaliates – just as Bianca enters with Charlie.

Matt Bianca . . .

Bianca What have you done?

Matt

I took her out to celebrate / Felt like myself again	**Aly** Mum
	Bianca You take
As if the clouds were lifting	**Aly** Please
	Bianca My child
I had sunlight in my brain	**Aly** Dad
	Bianca You don't Even phone

I'm sure your future's brighter

With a better man than me	**Aly** Don't
	Bianca How hard I try

So put me in this teapot And pour me	**Aly** Don't
	Bianca To make
Pour me out like tea	A home You break My heart

He is pouring tea all over his table. The police arrive, led by WPC Rook. The Waiters point out Matt.
   Matt picks up two cakes. The police arrest him, putting him in handcuffs.

Matt
Sooner or later
I had to mess it up
The sun's behind the clouds again

72

And empty is my cup
Somehow in my innards
There's a crazy laugh;
Why forego the cake of life?
Just share it –

The Waiters approach Matt as he sings.

Waiter You, sir, are an idiot

Matt

Have some on my behalf

*Matt covers the Waiters in cake. Chaos ensues, Aly a
still point in the middle of it.*

*Matt runs all over the restaurant, more manic than
ever. The police chase him. Bianca is chasing him too,
in anger. Luke is his right-hand man. The customers
love Matt and are cheering him on. The M.C. appears
in a giant teapot.*

Aly finds his surreal appearance a great relief.

Chorus

Sooner or later
You'll begin to see
That life is not a gambling site
And chances don't come free
Clubs are what you're hit with
Diamonds what you spend
Hearts are pain and happiness
And spades, they dig you
They dig you to your end

Interval.

Act Two

SEVEN

THE GARDEN OF LIVE FLOWERS

OVERTURE – GAME

*Ms Manxome is manipulating two-dimensional Alice
as she runs through the gardens. As she travels, in the
style of a platform game, Ms Manxome buys her red
shoes, a red dress, red hair and finally a crown. She
spends money, without caring. Ms Manxome is delighted
with Alice's new look.*

Alice appears in three dimensions.

SONG – ME

Ms Manxome
    I'm walking on a beam
    My euphoria's extreme
    Being here with me
    In this self-indulgent dream

Alice
    Me

Ms Manxome I'll renew and redeem
    I am once again a teen
    My senses all thaw
    I'm a melting ice cream

Alice
    Me

Ms Manxome
    I'm no longer alone

Alice
    Me

Ms Manxome

    Like a toenail all ingrown
    You and me are one
    Our future is the only one

Alice / Ms Manoxme

    Me
    It's me
    Me

*   Ms Manxome is riding around on her desk. She buys
    four pet playing cards. The three-dimensional cards
    come past her. She is having a heavenly time
    manipulating Alice.*

Ms Manxome

    Sharing every thought
    In this wonderful resort
    With me I can cavort
    And I have my full support

Alice

    Me

Ms Manxome

    I'm a vision in red

Alice

    A crimson thoroughbred
    Those who cross my path
    I am happy to behead

Alice

    Me

Ms Manxome

    I'm no longer alone
    Me

Alice

    Like a pickled kidney stone

You and me are one
My future is the only one

Ms Manxome
Me

Alice
It's me
Me

Meanwhile, down at the police station . . .
Interview room. WPC Rook has Matt and Bianca at the desk. Aly is holding Charlie.

SONG – HEARTLESS USELESS

WPC Rook
Now, be still until
My form I fill

Aly I know what actually happened

WPC Rook
Your name and address, sir

Matt Matt the Hat Hatton

WPC Rook
Explain this mess

Bianca Oh you are too much

WPC Rook
Communicate

Matt No, you're too much

WPC Rook
I am the law
Ignoring me's –

Aly I'm not ignoring you

WPC Rook
A fatal flaw

Bianca You bloody fool

WPC Rook
Madam, please refrain

Bianca What?

WPC Rook
While I ascertain

Bianca What?

WPC Rook
The important facts

Bianca Well, you don't know him

WPC Rook
The related acts
Did you just provoke?

Matt No

Aly No

Bianca Yes

WPC Rook
Or did you deck that bloke?
You're accused today

Matt Of what?

WPC Rook
Of assault and affray

Bianca
Oh you're such a foolish man

Matt Don't start

Bianca
Flush yourself down the pan

I just don't know what to say cos
You have turned my hair half grey now

WPC Rook I need to take your statement, sir

Matt
Well then let me take a bow

Bianca Keep it

Matt
Seriously, darling, I've begged
For mercy; oh how I've knelt! –

Both
Still reeling from the blows you dealt me

WPC Rook Your statement please

Aly slopes off. She lingers, listening painfully.

Matt	**Bianca**
You're heartless	Useless
Heartless	Useless
Like a bag of rusty nails	As a pair of dirty socks
Heartless	Useless
Throw me on the rocks	Drive me off the rails
	More like

Matt
You're like an icy hurricane
A blast of arctic breeze
I know I made a huge mistake
But when will you unfreeze?

Bianca
You say I'm ice? take my advice
And shape up if you dare

WPC Rook Sir?

Bianca
You're like another baby, Matt
You've used up all my care

Matt This is the clink, Charlie

WPC Rook I am trying to take your statement

Aly Take *my* statement. It was an accident

Bianca Will you wait over there, my love?

WPC Rook Can we get started?

Bianca
  You kept a secret life from me
  By gambling online –

WPC Rook Madam –

Matt
  I know and I've apologised
  And that's the bottom line!

WPC Rook Sir –

Matt
  Now if you can't get over it –

Bianca
  The fault here isn't mine! And

Both
  The tenderness I feel for you's
  In terminal decline

WPC Rook I miss my mum

Matt	**Bianca**
You're heartless	Useless
Heartless	Useless
Like a bag of rusty nails	As a pair of dirty socks
Heartless	Useless
Throw me on the rocks	Drive me off the rails
	More like

Matt
  I'm sure that I'm a nightmare

79

Bianca
I am full of human flaws

Both
But you're standing up in judgement
While I'm lying on the floor
While I'm lying on the floor

Matt	**Bianca**
You're heartless	Useless
Heartless	Useless
Like a bag of rusty nails	As a pair of dirty socks
Heartless	Useless
Throw me on the rocks	Drive me off the rails
	More like

WPC Rook (*over the final chorus*)
Be still until
My form I fill
Your name and address, sir
Explain this mess

Aly is getting more and more distressed by the argument.

Aly
Sooner or later
You'll begin to see
That I am only holding on to
Shreds of a family
We're a bunch of cracked-up fragments
We're made of broken glass

Her parents finally calm down.

Bianca Make sure they give you a lawyer

Matt I won't need one

Bianca Come on, Aly. There's nothing we can do here

Matt Don't you worry about a thing – justice will prevail

WPC Rook Always good to be an optimist, sir

Out on the street:

Aly Can I borrow your phone, Mum? I need to get online

Bianca Just be with me, can't you? Be here

Back in the wonder.land garden (and Ms Manxome's office), Alice and Ms Manxome are still swimming in Lake Me:

SONG – ME (REPRISE)

Alice
  Me

Ms Manxome
  I'm no longer alone

The avatars enter.

Mouse Hey, Alice

Humpty We found you

Ms Manxome
  Me

Alice
  Like a queen without a throne

Mouse Have you been missing me?

Dum and Dee start copying Alice's steps.

Ms Manxome
  / I'll never be outdone

Dodo What's she singing?

Alice
  For you are me and I'm the only one

The avatars join in with Alice's song – thinking that she is singing with and for them:

Ms Manxome
/ It's me

Alice
Me

Mouse That's right, Alice, it's all about me

Humpty I'm me

Mock Turtle I'm me too

Ms Manxome / Alice
It's me
Me

Dum I'm unique

Dee And so's she

The avatars' singing becoming more anarchic. They begin to take over the song.

Avatars
It's me me

Ms Manxome is deeply disturbed by them.

Ms Manxome What are they doing? Are they laughing at me?

Alice They're my friends

Ms Manxome They're a rabble

Alice Are they?

Ms Manxome They're stealing my song; they're destroying it

Alice You're destroying my song!

The avatars stop, surprised.

Humpty What's up?

Dum We were just having fun

Mock Turtle Have we upset you?

Mouse She's playing hard to get, that's what it is

Ms Manxome Don't be ridiculous

Humpty What's with the red, Alice?

Mouse You are so hot. I'm on fire

Dodo (*to Mouse*) Mate, dick

Dee Our dad says red is a slut colour

Alice How dare you!

The avatars are taken aback.

Dum *and* **Dee** Oooooooh

Dodo Alice, talk to us. We're your friends

Ms Manxome No they're not

Alice No you're not

Ms Manxome I'll tell you about friends

Dee Someone's got the hump

Ms Manxome One minute they're all affable and jolly and the next, they turn on you

Mouse Lady lumps

Ms Manxome They stab you in the back. They say things like:

Dum Someone's got a poker stuck up her botty

Ms Manxome You see? Friends are never friends. You're better off alone

Humpty Something's up, isn't it? You're different

Alice I'm better off alone

Mock Turtle No you're not

Mouse We're better off together. I'd let you explore my body

Ms Manxome Ugh!

Dodo Alice, he has base physical desires –

Mouse I want to touch your arse

Dodo Whereas I have difficult emotional sensations –

Ms Manxome Leave me alone!

Dodo Can I borrow your dress?

Ms Manxome I won't be laughed at!

Alice That's enough!

Alice pushes over the Mouse.

Mock Turtle Alice, they were only farting around

Ms Manxome Get rid of them

Alice Get out of this garden!

Humpty You have totally changed

Alice Get out, I said

Humpty You can't order us about

Alice Oh, yes I can

Ms Manxome I am your Head Teach— No . . .

Ms Manxome / Alice I am your Queen

Mock Turtle Since when?

Mouse You're a queen?

Dum and Dee Oooooh Your Majesty

84

Mock Turtle So, this is a monarchy?

Dodo I thought it was an anarchist collective

Humpty You're not a queen
   (*Singing.*) It's you

Ms Manxome Command them

Alice Leave my garden

> *The other avatars join in. They are all troubled by the change in Alice.*

Everyone
   It's you, you, you, you it's you

Ms Manxome Get them out of here!

Everyone
   You

Alice Get out of here

Everyone
   You

Alice I hate you

Everyone
   It's you, you, you, you, you

Ms Manxome Stop singing my song

Alice Shut up! Listen to me!

Everyone
   It's you, you, you, you, you, you

Ms Manxome Of course it's me

Everyone
   You

Alice
   It's me

Everyone
You

Ms Manxome
Me

Alice
Me

Everyone
You

Alice and Ms Manxome are driven away.

Humpty That's the trouble with these online games. You think you know someone and they just turn weird on you

Mock Turtle Yeah

Dee Yeah, maybe Alice is some forty-year-old

Dum Yeah, or some lonely old bag with cats

Dee Yeah

Dum Yeah

Mouse Maybe Alice is some guy who sits in his room and puts farts in bottles and gives them to his mum

Mock Turtle I really liked her

Avatars Yeah, yeah

Dodo Me too

EIGHT
THE WHITE QUEEN

Meanwhile, Aly is arriving back at home.

Bianca You missed a detention?

Aly Yeah but –

Bianca You were playing on your phone in the toilets during lesson time?

Aly Mum –

Bianca Confiscated – till the end of the year??

Aly It's completely unfair

SONG – GADGET

Bianca
Alice, what can I say?
I'm worried. I'm worried about you

Aly
I know but
It's my spellcheck; I was in the loos revising
And I didn't hear the bell go, which I think is
    unsurprising

Bianca Just tell me the truth!

Aly
All right, I'm being bullied. These girls are out for blood

Bianca What girls? Aly . . .

Aly
They're teasing me about my dad. They drag him
    through the mud

Bianca holds in her feelings about Matt.

See, you don't even care.
Ever since you broke us up, all you care about is Charlie!

Bianca
If there are bullies on your case then I'm so glad I know
Together we can make them stop – you needn't suffer so
But I broke us up? You say I care for Charlie more?

That's rubbish . . .
Why don't we go in and see your Head Teacher?

87

Aly No way. That's *crap*

Bianca Aly?

Aly

Now let's talk about what's really going on
Your rows with dad! – Cos you are in the wrong

Bianca We're going to park this

Aly

You've been blaming him for everything; you're
    totally uncaring

Bianca Don't push me

Aly

You never listen to me, Mum. I think that fact is glaring

Bianca Aly

Aly

You think you know it all but you're full of crap –

Bianca

I know what this reaction is; it's all about that *thing*

Aly What thing?

Bianca

That horrid little mobile that has truly sucked you in

Aly It's called a smartphone

Bianca

You're addicted to it, Aly; you're dependent, like a user
That gadget to you is like tequila to a boozer

Aly

That's crap
That's crap, you're talking crap right to my face

Bianca

So before another day goes by here's what we're going
    to do

Except for homework, games and the internet are
   banned for you

Aly
No way

Bianca
Banned from your room
Banned from this flat
Banned that is that

Aly
That's crap

Charlie vomits all over Aly. A deluge.

Oh that baby is disgusting. He's a little pig

Bianca How dare you call him a little pig? He can't help it!

Bianca takes Charlie.

I don't want to argue, Aly. I'm just trying to hold things
together. Clear this up, then get ready for bed. I'm going
to sort out the baby. Then we're going to talk

Come on Charlie
Poor little Charlie
You're my man

Aly cleans up the vomit.

SONG – EVERYONE LOVES CHARLIE

Aly
Everyone loves Charlie
Everyone loves Charlie
Everyone loves Charlie
Everyone loves Charlie

Aly cleans herself up.

Most babies they are lovely
But not Charlie – he's a pain

89

Nobody else can see it and
I should be slain for saying it
I'm horrible
And yes perhaps it's wrong,
Cos he's my little brother;
He'll be here my whole life

Elsewhere, Bianca is playing with Charlie.

Bianca
Everyone loves Charlie
Everyone loves Charlie

Matt is in his cell, gazing at a picture of Charlie.

Matt / Bianca
Everyone loves Charlie
Everyone loves Charlie

Aly
I wish that things could be
Just like they were before –
Mum and me and Dad
Me, my mum and dad
No more
Everyone loves Charlie
Charlie is the man
Everyone loves Charlie

Aly puts on her hoody. She steals some money from Bianca's purse.

It's hard when you grow up, Charlie
And you're not so gorgeous any more
You'll find that your family's hardly
Any consolation – you're insecure
So why should I stay here, Charlie,
When every day it feels like I'm at war?
I'm telling you it's quite lonely
When you're the only one who gets adored

But

    I've found a place
    Where I feel strong
    A place to be
    When things go wrong
    I'm going to go
    Where I belong

Aly *and* **Chorus**
    Everyone loves Charlie

Aly is outside. The whole night sky is full of images of Charlie.

Chorus
    Everyone loves Charlie   He is the man
    Everyone loves Charlie   We love him so

Aly Yeah, all right

Chorus
    Everyone loves Charlie   He is the man
    Everyone loves Charlie   We love him so

Aly Give me a break
Shut up

Chorus
    Everyone loves Charlie

Aly is travelling through the dark streets. We see passers-by and everyone in the world – all loving Charlie.

NINE
THE RED QUEEN

Late in the evening. Aly arrives at a dingy internet café.

Cashier You got ten minutes before we close

Aly is finally online. Ms Manxome is arming Alice.

M.C. Access to avatar denied

Aly What?

Ms Manxome (*buying Alice a sword*) A sword

A scroll-down list of weapons appears. Miss Manxome buys one.

Aly Why won't it recognise my password?

M.C. Vorpal Slayer Broadsword, ninety-nine pence

Ms Manxome Buy

Alice (*taking the sword*) A sword

Aly 'Already in Use'?

Ms Manxome We will have order

Aly Alice!

No one in wonder.land can hear Aly.

Ms Manxome / Alice
I'm going to have this garden all to myself

Aly What are you talking about?

Ms Manxome Ready your sword

Alice What for?

Ms Manxome Battle

Alice But they're my friends; we know each other's secrets

Ms Manxome Secrets are weapons too. Use them

Humpty Have you seen what she's doing?

Mock Turtle What on earth does she want with that?

Dodo Autocratic oppression

Mouse No, it's penis envy, Phallic Alice

Dum She wants to slice us

Dee Like cake

Alice turns on the avatars. The Mouse nervously faces
her, the other avatars peering around him.
    Aly interjects with 'Alice, Stop, This isn't me!'

Ms Manxome / Alice
    In this virtual world where you play
    Your delinquency I'll keep at bay
    You children will have to revere and obey
    For those who do wrong, it is punishment day
    My rod and my lash they are coming your way
    I've abandoned control of my urges to flay –
    The Red Queen
    The Red Queen is coming to stay

Aly The Red Queen? Alice, what are you doing?

Alice
    O children, O children
    Listen to me

    Alice swishes her sword. The avatars cry out and
    scatter.

Aly (*realising*) It's Miss Manxome . . .

Alice
    The Red Queen is going
    To reign over thee

Aly It has to be her!

Alice
    This world is not real
    So it's morally free
    O children

Aly Those are my friends!

93

Alice damages the Mouse.

Listen to me

Mouse I'm glitching!

Aly How dare you take my avatar!

Ms Manxome / Alice
In my virtual kingdom I'll rule
Who cares if you think that I'm cruel?
I'm free from the boundaries enforced by my school
My innermost nature emerges and you'll
Agree that it's shining and hard like a jewel
My sovereign authority's making me drool
The Red Queen is *me* – and she's cool

Aly Alice is me – you've stolen me

Ms Manxome / Alice
O children O children
Listen to me

Aly You stay away from my friends

Ms Manxome / Alice
The Red Queen is going
To reign over thee

Aly No way! You're twisted.

Ms Manxom / Alice
This world is not real

Humpty We have to stand up to her!

Ms Manxome / Alice
So it's morally free
O children –

Humpty I don't like you

Ms Manxome Like me?

Alice I don't want to be liked

Ms Manxome / Alice
   I want to be *obeyed*

Humpty Well I think you should fuck off

   Shocked intakes of breath. Ms Manxome draws herself up.

Ms Manxome It's time to let rip, Alice

Alice No wonder girls hate you, you boring prat

Ms Manxome (*delighted*) listen

Alice You're twisted; you wear girl's bras

Ms Manxome
   Listen

Alice Pizza Face, stay in your box

Ms Manxome
   Listen

Alice Why don't you starve and die?

Ms Manxome
   Listen

Alice No wonder your parents hit you

   Alice bursts Humpty.

Ms Manxome / Alice
   Listen to me

   Ms Manxome is thrilled; she is laughing, a great release in her. The other avatars are appalled.

M.C. Warning: deletion
No extreme malice
AllyPally32, your avatar is in danger of deletion

   Aly comes out of the game.

Aly
O someone
O someone
Listen to me
She's stolen
My only sanctuary

Cashier You got five minutes before we close

Aly I'm shaking
My hands are shaking
What can I do?
Mum – No . . .
Dad – No! . . .

Cashier You've got four –

Aly I need more time – please!

Cashier You've got four minutes before we close

Aly (*inspired*) Zombie Swarm. Luke!

Aly types. Luke appears, fighting a throng of zombies.

Luke

Luke Aly, where have you been? I've been waiting for you

Aly I'm in a cyber café; my mum's banned the internet

Luke Seriously?

Aly That teacher who took my phone – Miss Manxome. She's been in my game. She's messed with Alice

Luke Your avatar?

Aly Alice is *me*. She's done it to me –

Luke Done what?

Aly She's *corrupted* me –

Luke Miss Manxome?

Aly Like – she's the Head Teacher! We're supposed to trust her! She's come into my game and she's hurting people, like really damaging us

Luke (*killing a zombie*) That's so wrong

Aly I can't get in there. She's got my passwords and everything

Luke OK, one second

He gives her a bat.

Take this

Aly Luke! Luke!

Luke is fighting zombies. Aly fights them too – and decks a couple.

Luke We'll sort it out first thing tomorrow. We can sneak into her office and get your phone back –

Aly I need my phone back now. She's got a deletion warning. Alice will be destroyed

Luke Seriously?

Aly She's at the school. I'm going to stop her

Luke Wait – wait – I'll come and meet you

Aly Will you?

Luke Course I will

Aly I'll be at the gates. I knew you'd help me. I just knew it

Meanwhile, in the police station . . . Matt is sitting, alone.

Matt

It's hardly odd that sometimes
I'm found sitting like a freak
Alone, pretending I am with someone
Not closed in a room, in these locks and chains
Hoping joy is born of love
Not money and not wine
And that Eden's waiting somewhere
In its beautiful design

Sooner or later
You'll begin to see
That I am only holding on to
Shreds of a family
I'm a cluster of mere fragments
I'm made of broken glass

Bianca is alone in Aly's bedroom.

Bianca

It's hardly odd that sometimes
I'm found wishing all alone
That my arms were strong enough to keep at bay
All the forces of chaos that come our way
Hoping joy is born of love
Through fragility we shine
And Eden's waiting somewhere
In its beautiful design

Bianca / Matt

Sooner or later
You'll begin to see
That I am only holding on to
Shreds of a family
I'm a cluster of mere fragments
I'm made of broken glass

Bianca goes to Aly's room.

Bianca Aly, let's not fall out. All I want is for us to be a family again

She opens the door. The room is empty.

Aly?
Alice? . . .

TEN
QUEEN ALICE

Luke and Aly are greeting each other at the school gates.

Aly Can you give me a leg up?

Luke Are you going in – just like that?

Aly Yeah

Luke You're going to rob the school?

Aly It's not robbing; it's my phone. Miss Manxome's the thief – she's stolen Alice

Aly starts to climb.

Luke Aly . . . you should tell someone where you are

Aly I've told you

Luke Think this through, will you?

Aly I have

She climbs higher.

Luke This is breaking and entering – an actual crime

Aly What Miss Manxome's done is a crime

Luke To you and me. But if you get caught, no one will understand. It's just a game

Aly No it's not – I have been *invaded*. She's damaging people. Come on

Aly jumps down on the other side of the wall.

Luke You're a lot like your dad

Aly Don't slag off my dad

Luke I'm not; he's really great. He doesn't care what anyone thinks. But it gets him in a lot of trouble. This is brave, Aly, but it's really stupid. Please don't do it

Aly I need your help

Luke Not this way

Aly Seriously? You won't come with me?

Luke shakes his head.

Well . . . Some friend you turn out to be

Aly runs off into the school. Luke types into his smartphone.

SONG – FABULOUS (REPRISE)

M.C.
Oh press OK
Fabulous

The M.C. plays the tune of 'Fabulous' on a melodica under the following scenes.

Luke Putting out the word
Come to wonder.land. See the real Ms Manxome – online thief

From the network:

Kitty What's going on?

Mary Ann What's up?

Dinah Spill

Luke Miss Manxome's playing on a confiscated phone. She's stolen Alice Hatton's avatar –

Kitty That's so wrong

Dinah She's messing with our phones?

Mary Ann Privacy invasion

Ms Manxome I'm going to annihilate you all

Meanwhile at the police station:

Bianca I don't know what's happened

Matt Aly's gone missing?

Bianca We had a row

Matt This is our fault; all we do is row

Bianca When I went to make it up with her she was gone

Matt Where on earth can she be?

Bianca I don't know.

She gives Matt her smartphone.

But this is where we'll find her

Matt I haven't touched one of these in months

In wonderland:

Dum When she comes back, we're going to be ready

Dee Yeah, this is war

Humpty Yeah

Dodo No

Mock Turtle I don't want to fight

Humpty But she's a psycho

Dee Yeah

Dum Yeah

Dodo I'm a pacifist

Mock Turtle Yeah

Mouse We have to defend ourselves

Avatars Yeah, no, yeah, no, yeah

Back on the network:

Luke Alice is breaking into the school right now to get her phone back

Kitty Seriously?

Mary Ann No way

Dinah That is EPIC

Luke Spread the word

Get it out there

And at the police station:

WPC Rook We've got our patrol cars out looking for her. I'm sure she'll turn up

Bianca We've found her

Matt Not geographically – but she's here

Bianca He's hacked into her game

WPC Rook Is that legal?

Matt There's her username. That's our Alice, there

Ms Manxome / Alice I am going to have order in this garden. It'll be a teenage-free zone. I'm going to *wipe you out*

M.C. PRESS OK

Suddenly, the White Rabbit appears, standing between Alice and the avatars.

Ms Manxome There's that funny white bunny

Alice Hello, Big Ears

Ms Manxome What does it want?

Alice He wants us to follow him.

Ms Manxome Why?

Alice You know why; we're on a quest. Where are you taking me now?

The White Rabbit shakes his head.

Ms Manxome It isn't going anywhere

Alice Why aren't you moving?

The White Rabbit nods.

Ms Manxome Come on, you flop-eared loon

Ms Manxome / Alice Get out of my way. Move

Aly takes hold of the phone.

Aly / Alice No, you move. Get out of my game

Bianca That's Alice –

Ms Manxome What are you doing here?

Aly / Alice You stole Alice

Ms Manxome I am Alice

As they struggle over the phone, Alice is fighting with herself

Ms Manxome / Alice Give that phone to me

Aly / Alice It's mine

Matt She's fighting with someone

Kitty Alice must be in there

Dinah Violence

Ms Manxome / Alice Let it GO

*As she pulls the phone, Alice swishes the sword –
killing the White Rabbit. In wonderland, there is
pandemonium.*

M.C. Warning: deletion
No extreme malice

Avatars What's she done? She killed him. She's wrecked
our game. She's a monster, *etc.*

Bianca / Where are you, Alice?

Matt / What's happening to you?

Mary Ann / Ugh. Gross

Dinah / Get everyone online – now

Kitty / Hashtag live beheading

M.C. You have broken our term and condition

Ms Manxome Now look what you've done

Aly That wasn't my fault

Aly / Alice She's stolen my identity. Please, let me
explain –

M.C. You are guilty of malicious destruction. You will
now be deleted from the game

Aly / Alice No, no it wasn't me

M.C. But you are Alice

Aly / Alice No, I am Alice

Ms Manxome / Alice I'm Alice

Aly / Alice I'm Alice

Ms Manxome (*getting the phone back*) I am the only
Alice that matters

M.C. Then the question is –

M.C.
Who are you?

Aly / Alice
I'm Alice

M.C.
Who are you?

Ms Manxome / Alice
I'm Alice

Avatars
Alice, who are you?

*This exchange continues as Manxome and Aly struggle
for the phone under the following:*

Girls
Go on Alice, get Miss Manxome and you're sorted
Cos if you can prove she stole your game she's
absolutely thwarted
You're still flabby round the edges and you're a crazy
weirdo
But you're getting loads of followers; and you're
trending like a hero

Avatars
Who is Alice? Who is Alice? She keeps changing
First she's friendly and she's funny now her temper
is ablazing
Is she violent, full of malice? Her behaviour is deranging
Does she need a dose of psychiatric rearranging?

Matt
Aly my darling girl
If you can hear me, you shine –
Here's how much I love you

Bianca
I once held you in my arms

Matt
I love you with a scattergun of splurging love

Bianca
A tiny little bird

Matt
You're the one still point in the chaos
My lighthouse

Bianca
My dear one

Matt
My bright beam

Bianca
My one girl

Matt
My angel
Like an earthquake shaking my heart

Bianca / Matt
You can fly. Light up the night with your smile

Luke appears in wonder.land.

Aly Luke

Luke I'm here

Dodo Who's that?

Luke I'm here

Mary Ann He's hot

Kitty He's cute

Dinah He's Luke

Ms Manxome Luke Laprel

Aly / Alice Luke, you're in my game!

Luke Are you in Miss Manxome's office?

Aly / Alice Yes

Matt Manxome?

Bianca She's at the school

WPC Rook Come on

Matt Aly, we're coming

Luke Give Aly back her phone

Ms Manxome / Alice Or what?

Luke Or this

Some zombies appear.

Ms Manxome Who are they?

Luke They're my zombies

Ms Manxome / Alice
Off with their heads!

Alice fights Luke.
Ms Manxome and Aly struggle for the phone.
The avatar chorus repeats:

Avatars
Who is Alice? who is Alice? She keeps changing
First she's friendly and she's funny now her temper
   is a-blazing
Is she violent, full of malice? Her behaviour is deranging
Does she need a dose of psychiatric rearranging?

*The zombies attack the schoolgirls. The avatars fight
off the zombies.*
The girls' chorus repeats:

Girls
Go on, Alice, get Miss Manxome and you're sorted
Cos if you can prove she stole your game she's
    absolutely thwarted
You're still flabby round the edges and you're a crazy
    weirdo
But you're getting loads of followers; and you're
    trending like a hero

*At the end of the choruses Ms Manxome has Aly's head
in her paper guillotine and is about to behead her.*
    *Alice has Luke on the end of her blade and is about
to kill him. The lines between what's real and unreal
are completely blurred.*
    Aly gets hold of the phone.

Chorus
Who

Aly Alice, don't. I love Luke

Chorus
Are

Alice I love you, Luke

Alice snogs Luke. Luke is completely freaked out.

Aly Not like that!

Luke That is weird

Ms Manxome It's disgusting (*To Alice, grabbing the
phone.*) Kill him!

Alice kills Luke. Luke dies.

Aly Stop! (*To Ms Manxome.*) You just killed my friend –

*The zombies drag Luke away. Alice begins to
malfunction.*

Alice

    I'm Alice you dimwit.
    You can see perfectly well who I am
    I'm epic
    Who told you I was lonely?
    CURIOUS CURIOUS
    I know they shun me in the staff room
    I FEEL LIKE I'M BELONGING
    You're destroying my song
    THIS IS AMAZING THIS IS WONDERFUL
    How dare you
    I'M FALLING DOWN
    I am your Queen
    You can say anything to me
    NEVER NEVER BE FOUND
    Why don't you starve and die?
    ME
    I hate you
    I'm going to wipe you out

M.C. Your avatar has been corrupted. It will be deleted in ten

Chorus

    You

Aly You're right. Alice has been corrupted

M.C. Nine

Ms Manxome Don't delete her!

Aly (*to Ms Manxome*) I have to

M.C. Eight

Alice You have to delete me

M.C. Seven

Aly Don't be afraid, Alice

Ms Manxome Please

M.C. Six

Alice I'm not afraid of anything

Ms Manxome I am!

M.C. Five

Alice You know who you are

M.C. Four

Aly I know who I am

Ms Manxome She's me

M.C. Three

Ms Manxome Don't take her away

M.C. Two

Ms Manxome I'm all alone

M.C. Nearly there

Ms Manxome No!

M.C. One

Aly Thank you, Alice

Alice I have finished my quest

Alice disintegrates into thousands of tiny fragments.

Ms Manxome You've destroyed her

Aly You've destroyed yourself

Luke enters, filming with his smartphone. Aly and Ms Manxome are unaware of him. But everyone online sees Ms Manxome.

Ms Manxome I'm calling the police. I have you for breaking and entering and attempted burglary –

Aly You put my head in your guillotine

Ms Manxome I won't rest until you're expelled from my school. You should be caned. You should be flogged – what is that?

She sees Luke's phone.

Luke I put the word out online, Ms Manxome. Now I'm live-streaming you

Aly Luke! . . .

Ms Manxome (*turns, seeing him*) You're what?

Luke Say hi

Bianca and Matt enter. Matt holds Charlie.

Bianca Aly

Matt My darling

Bianca (*advancing on Ms Manxome*) Is this the cow who stole your avatar?

Ms Manxome I have nothing to be ashamed of

Bianca Oh yes you do

Matt You stole our child's identity

Aly Mum

Bianca But Aly was amazing. She fought you back with such dignity. Whereas I'm just going to punch your poxy lights out

Matt My love –

Matt holds Bianca back, as WPC Rook enters.

Ms Manxome Officer, I am under attack from this ghastly problem family! First the daughter, now the mother

WPC Rook So this family are attacking you?

Ms Manxome Their child has broken in and run amok in my school. They are the kind of people that every teacher dreads

Bianca Then dread this. I'm going to make sure you lose your job

Ms Manxome How?

Aly You played my game. You messed up Alice

Ms Manxome I played a game; is that my crime?

Aly You killed the White Rabbit – you killed Luke

Luke Yeah

Ms Manxome Luke Laprel is lounging limpidly before your eyes

WPC Rook So this girl broke in?

Ms Manxome Exactly

Luke I've got her on film saying Aly should be flogged

Ms Manxome It was self-defence. The girl attacked me. She was trying to steal school property

WPC Rook Now theft is a serious matter

Bianca What?

Ms Manxome Absolutely right. There are youth detention centres for delinquents like this

Aly You're joking

WPC Rook The law is the law

Bianca The law is an idiot

WPC Rook I'm going to have to take you down to the station, miss

Bianca Over my dead body

Aly This can't be happening

Ms Manxome You see? I am crimeless

Matt Except . . . you stole Aly's money

Ms Manxome Nonsense

WPC Rook I beg your pardon?

Matt You bought a Vorpal Slayer Broadsword for 99p and you spent £5.83 on Pet Playing Cards and Red Accessories

Ms Manxome That wasn't real money

Matt Yes it was. There's the evidence

Aly You're brilliant, Dad

WPC Rook So you took this child's phone and spent her money?

Matt She certainly did

WPC Rook Then I'm afraid you're going to have to come with me

Luke You're trending, Miss Manxome. The local paper's following you now

Ms Manxome Then let them print this:
I'm a beacon, I'm a shining light
And I'm not contrite
You're a blight, you're trite
You offend my sight
I pity your plight
And everything anyone says about me is shite

WPC Rook Why don't you come and explain it to us, Madam?

Ms Manxome

I am right, I'm right, I'm right in every single thing
I've done. That's why I'm held in esteem, why my
trophies all gleam, why my school is supreme; other
teachers just dream of one day singing my song

Family

She's wrong, she's wrong, she's wrong in every single
thing she's done, she's really wrong, she's so wrong

Ms Manxome (*to Aly and Luke*)

You traitors to the school. You are lumpen brutes and
you deserve to fail – just like your miserable, issue-
ridden, job-seeking, sandal-wearing parents

Bianca I don't wear sandals

Ms Manxome

Father warned me all about them

WPC Rook You can tell us everything down at the
station

Ms Manxome

He told me I was right every day so I know they're a
mess. They will never progress; they're a shambles,
they're waste, they have unrefined taste and I've
ached in my efforts; I've bled.
So go home and fail. When your future's unveiled it's
the Poundshop or jail and that hits the nail on
he head

WPC Rook If you'd just come along with us now

Everyone (*under the following*)

She's wrong, she's wrong, she's wrong in every single
thing she says. She's really wrong, like an out-of-tune
song or a very bad pong or a man in a thong, we've
known all along – she's wrong

Ms Manxome

You're dead. I hate you. I'd chop off your head like
that bunny. You think that I'm funny? You're wasting
state money; a drain on all we invest

(*To WPC Rook*.) They'll flunk every test. They're a pain
in my chest; they would make me depressed if
I wasn't utterly sure I was blessed

How dare you suggest that I'm wrong; I protest. Do
you think that I'm keeping my feelings repressed?
They're free, like wild horses. I am special forces
and you lot will never be best

I'm the cream of the crop, you're a miserable flop, I'll
expand on the theme of my leadership dream; I am
held in esteem and my trophies all gleam, so my
school is supreme and I am right

Everyone

She's held in esteem while her trophies all gleam and
her school is supreme, other teachers just dream to
be held in esteem while their trophies all gleam but
she's oh so wrong

*Ms Manxome and the WPC Rook go. Aly is reunited
with her family.*

Bianca Never ever run off in the night again

Aly Sorry

Bianca I'm sorry too, baby

Matt I promise that from now on I will be the poster-
bloke for dads. I'm going run Dad workshops – I'm going
to write the Dad Manual –

Aly Dad –

Matt I know – I'm completely mad

Aly Yeah. But all the best people are. (*To Luke*.) Sorry
about that kiss.

Luke That's OK. My avatar's straight.

Aly Really?

Luke No. You've got to say something, Aly, for your followers. They want to know how you feel, after bringing down an unhinged Head Teacher?

SONG – SECRETS (REPRISE)

Aly
I really don't know what I'm feeling
Perhaps it's just hard to define
A kind of a glow
Something powerful and slow
An assurance I know my own mind
I know that my family is right by my side
Though we're apart we are so strongly tied

And now I've done talking
The day has begun

Alice
In a great rush of freedom
The river will run

Aly Alice is still with me, you know. It's like she's rumbling in my stomach

Bianca Food; that's what we need. Matt . . . why don't you come and have breakfast with us?

Matt I'd love to but . . . I have to be somewhere

Bianca It's all right; it's just breakfast

Matt Seriously, I've got a court appearance. The magistrates

Bianca Oh . . . Oh yeah

Aly (*to Charlie*) What do you reckon, cabbage-pants? Shall we go and stand up for our dad in front of the magistrates?

The M.C. and the avatars enter.

M.C.
www dot wonder.land

Avatars
Come back, Alice

We see the avatars in wonder.land.

M.C.
www dot wonder.land

Avatars
Alice come back

M.C.
www dot wonder.land

Luke
Are you gonna go?

Aly
Blimey, I dunno
I won't get very far
I got no avatar

M.C.
So
Who do you want to be?

Aly
Nobody else but me
I'm Alice unashamedly
Feels wonderful in my own skin
I don't want blonde, I don't need thin.

M.C.
Dot

Aly
I wanna be a girl

M.C.
www dot wonder.land

Aly
Cos I'm taking on the world

M.C.
www dot wonder.land

Luke
When something isn't right
You'll fight

Aly
Take it on the chin
With friends I'll always win

Avatars
Come and see us, Alice
We've respawned the Rabbit

Aly
I'd love to come and visit
But Mum has banned online

Bianca
Not banned forever, is it?
Just don't waste all your time

M.C.
www dot wonder.land

Everyone
I want to be a girl
Taking on the world

M.C.
www dot wonder.land

Everyone
When something isn't right
Not afraid to fight

M.C.
www.wonder.land

Everyone
We're not stupid
Pretty lucid

Perhaps it's causing damage to the cells within our
   brain
We lose the world around us as we steer through this
   domain
We sail past trolls and strangers and the landscape
   can be dark
But if this is the future, we're not going to disembark

This vivid world is
Slowly unfurling
My heart is blazing
Life is amazing
 www dot

Aly
I want to be this girl

M.C.
Fabulous

The End.